A Guide for Using

The Lion, the Witch and the Wardrobe

in the Classroom

Based on the novel written by C.S. Lewis

This guide written by Michael Shepherd

Illustrated By Keith Vasconcelles

Teacher Created Resources, Inc.
6421 Industry Way
Westminster, CA 92683
www.teachercreated.com

ISBN: 978-1-55734-409-0

©*1992 Teacher Created Resources, Inc.*
Reprinted, 2007
Made in U.S.A.

Table of Contents

Introduction

A good book can touch our lives like a good friend. Within its pages are words and characters that can inspire us to achieve our highest ideals. We can turn to it for companionship, recreation, comfort and guidance. It can also give us a cherished story to hold in our hearts forever.

In Literature Units, great care has been taken to select books that are sure to become good friends!

Teachers who use this unit will find the following features to supplement their own valuable ideas.

- Sample Lesson Plans

- Pre-reading Activities

- A Biographical Sketch and Picture of the Author

- A Book Summary

- Vocabulary Lists and Suggested Vocabulary Activities

- Chapters grouped for study, with each section including:

  — *quizzes*

  — *hands-on projects*

  — *cooperative learning activities*

  — *cross-curriculum connections*

  — *extensions into the reader's own life*

- Post-Reading Activities

- Book Report Ideas

- Research Ideas

- A Culminating Activity

- Three Different Options for Unit Tests

- Bibliography

- Answer Key

We are confident this unit will be a valuable addition to your planning, and we hope your students will increase the circle of "friends" they have in books as you use our ideas!

Sample Lesson Plan

Each of the lessons suggested below can take from one to several days to complete.

LESSON 1

- Introduce and complete some or all of the pre-reading activities found on page 5.
- Read "About the Author" with your students. (page 6)
- Introduce the vocabulary for SECTION 1. (page 8)
- Ask students to find definitions.

LESSON 2

- Read chapters 1 through 4. As you read, place the vocabulary words in the context of the story and discuss their meanings.
- Choose a vocabulary activity. (page 9)
- Discuss rainy day activities. (page 11)
- Act out a Narnia scene. (page 12)
- List and describe villains in literature. (page 13)
- Begin "Reading Response Journals." (page 14)
- Administer SECTION 1 quiz. (page 10)
- Introduce the vocabulary for SECTION 2. (page 8)
- Ask students to find definitions.

LESSON 3

- Read Chapters 5 through 8. Place the vocabulary words in context and discuss their meanings.
- Choose a vocabulary activity. (page 9)
- Play true/false game. (page 16)
- Discuss beavers fact and fantasy. (page 17)
- Practice logical thinking. (page 18)
- Discuss personal reputations. (page 19)
- Administer SECTION 2 quiz. (page 15)
- Introduce the vocabulary for SECTION 3. page 8)
- Ask students to find definitions.

LESSON 4

- Read chapters 9 through 11. Place the vocabulary words in context and discuss their meaning.
- Choose a vocabulary activity. (page 9)
- Make candy. (page 21)
- Research witches in history. (page 22)
- Compare good and evil rulers. (page 23)

LESSON 4 *(cont.)*

- Discuss temptation. (page 24)
- Administer SECTION 3 quiz. (page 20)
- Introduce the vocabulary for SECTION 4. (page 8)
- Ask students to find definitions.

LESSON 5

- Read chapters 12 through 14. Place the vocabulary words in context and discuss their meanings.
- Choose a vocabulary activity. (page 9)
- Collect information about heroes today. (page 26)
- Make a Narnia chess game. (page 27)
- Create the Stone Table mural. (page 28)
- Discuss ways to rescue others. (page 29)
- Administer SECTION 4 quiz. (page 25)
- Introduce the vocabulary for SECTION 5. (page 8)
- Ask students to find definitions.

LESSON 6

- Read chapters 15 through 17. Place the vocabulary words in context and discuss their meanings.
- Choose a vocabulary activity. (page 9)
- Construct a castle. (page 31)
- Discuss what you would do as king or queen. (page 32)
- Research lions. (page 33)
- Discuss ways to help people. (page 34)
- Administer SECTION 5 quiz. (page 30)

LESSON 7

- Discuss any questions your students have about the story. (page 35)
- Assign book report and research projects. (pages 36 and 37)
- Begin work on a culminating activity. (pages 38-41)

LESSON 8

- Administer Unit Tests: 1, 2, and/or 3. (pages 42, 43, and 44)
- Discuss the test answers and possibilities.
- Discuss the students' enjoyment of the book.
- Provide a list of related reading for your students. (page 45)

4

Before the Book

Before you begin reading *The Lion, the Witch and the Wardrobe* with your students, do some pre-reading activities to stimulate interest and enhance comprehension. Here are some activities that might work well in your class.

1. Predict what the story might be about just by hearing the title.

2. Predict what the story might be about just by looking at the cover illustration.

3. Find out if your students have ever heard of C.S. Lewis, and if they know anything about his personal life or his writing.

4. Answer these questions:

    • Are you interested in:

        — stories of fantasy and magic?

        — struggles between good and evil?

        — wicked witches that cast spells?

        — sacrifices one hero makes to save someone else?

    • Would you ever:

        — lie just to make yourself look good?

        — like to sit on a throne in a castle?

        — fight against a wicked queen?

        — forgive someone who was your enemy?

    • Have you ever imagined a fantasy world? Describe what it is like.

5. Work in groups or as a class to create your own fantasy storybook.

About the Author

C.S. Lewis was born on November 29, 1898, in Belfast, Ireland. His father was a lawyer. He attended various schools and was privately tutored before entering University College in Oxford, England. Wounded in World War I, he returned to Oxford, then Cambridge, as a professor of Medieval and Renaissance English literature.

Although he wrote many books for scholars, most people know Dr. Lewis through reading his books dealing with Christianity. Reared an Anglican Christian, he became an atheist in his teens for personal and philosophical reasons and did not return to Christianity until his early thirties. After rediscovering the truths of his faith, he began to share them in new and creative ways in his books.

Mere Christianity (1952) is a collection of radio talks he made for the British Broadcasting Corporation. *The Screwtape Letters* (1942) is his most popular book. It consists of letters of advice from the devil Screwtape to his nephew, Wormwood, on how to tempt and destroy a young Christian convert. *The Great Divorce* (1945) describes a bus trip from hell to heaven. His *Peralandra* (1943) trilogy is a science fiction account of the cosmic struggle between good and evil.

"My father bought all the books he read and never got rid of any of them . . . In the seemingly endless rainy afternoons I took volume after volume from the shelves." Even as a boy, Lewis enjoyed writing fantasy books of his own in an attic room of his house. "I wrote about chivalrous mice and rabbits who rode out in complete mail to kill not giants but cats." From a childhood immersed in books and writing came a life-long habit of writing.

The Narnia Chronicles for children were published from 1950 to 1956. *The Lion, the Witch and the Wardrobe, The Magician's Nephew, The Last Battle* and other books in the series retell the Christian story in a fairy tale form. For Lewis, the "fantasy" world of Narnia is often more real than in the world we live in because there, in Narnia, the struggle between good and evil is made very clear. Lewis died on November 22, 1963, the same day U.S. President John F. Kennedy was assassinated.

Quotations for this biographical sketch were taken from "C.S. Lewis," *Something About the Author*, Volume 13, page 132.

The Lion, the Witch and the Wardrobe

By C.S. Lewis

(Macmillan, 1950)

Peter, Susan, Edmund, and Lucy are visiting an old Professor in the country in order to avoid the air raids in London. Living in a huge old historic mansion is a new adventure for all of the children. The problem appears when Lucy, the youngest of the four brothers and sisters, is playing hide-and-seek and discovers another world, a world of fauns, witches, and magic, in the back of an old wardrobe. None of the other children believe her.

In the other world, Narnia, Lucy meets a faun, Mr. Tumnus, who admits to her that he is working for the White Witch. Tumnus has been assigned the job of finding and turning in "Sons of Adam" and "Daughters of Eve." Charmed by Lucy, he does not turn her in to the Witch. Meanwhile, Lucy's brother Edmund has found his way into Narnia, too, and has been told by the Witch (who claims to be Queen of Narnia) to bring in his brother and sisters. When he does this, says the Witch, she will give him more Turkish Delight, an enchanted candy, and will make Edmund King of Narnia.

Back in the mansion, Edmund lies to the others about having been in Narnia. He is eventually found out when all four children enter the wardrobe together. They find out that Mr. Tumnus has been taken captive by the Witch and his cave had been ransacked for not arresting Lucy. The children decide to try to help Tumnus, meet a family of beavers hostile to the Witch, and wind up fighting on the side of the forces of Aslan, a lion, the true King of Narnia.

Aslan's victory is not without some uncertainties, as when Aslan allows the Witch and her followers to kill him so that they will let Edmund (who acted as a traitor) go free. Yet the four do conquer with Aslan and rule on four thrones in Narnia at the castle called Cair Paravel. In the end, they find themselves back at the mansion with the Professor.

Vocabulary Lists

On this page are vocabulary lists which correspond to each sectional grouping of chapters. Vocabulary activity ideas can be found on page 9 of this book.

SECTION 1
Chapters 1-4

wardrobe	enchanted
housekeeper	batty
Adam	hissing
scarlet	explore
hoax	London
sledge	Eve
dwarf	imaginary
splendid	row
passages	inquisitive
muffler	parcels
distress	tongs
dominions	heather

SECTION 2
Chapters 5-8

faun	superior
enemies	secret police
handkerchief	camphor
beckoned	lamppost
disposal	fraternizing
sightseers	beasts
festoons	consideration
premises	earnestly
prophecy	reign

SECTION 3
Chapters 9-11

magic	centaur
shield	mysterious
laburnums	conversation
stammered	quiver
reindeer	delicious
Father Christmas	reckoned
cinema	schemes
sorcerer	ventured
mere	gloating
spectacles	eerie
solemn	vermin
repulsive	

SECTION 4
Chapters 12-14

kingfisher	bluebells
pavilion	awkward
victim	stump
solemn	ogres
triumph	resistance
prophecy	glades
dispute	summon
offense	shudder
treachery	shrill
forfeit	savage
perish	siege
dismay	

SECTION 5
Chapters 15-17

miserable	ghost
incantation	statues
giant	stag
muzzle	vile
traitor	apparently
nibbling	prodigious
battlements	concealed
wand	dungeon

Vocabulary Activity Ideas

You can help your students learn and retain the vocabulary in *The Lion, the Witch and the Wardrobe* by providing them with interesting vocabulary activities. Here are a few ideas to try.

❑ People of all ages like to make and solve puzzles. Ask your students to make their own **Crossword Puzzles** or **Wordsearch Puzzles** using the vocabulary words from the story.

❑ Challenge your students to a **Vocabulary Bee**. This is similar to a spelling bee, but in addition to spelling each word correctly, the game participants must correctly define the words as well.

❑ Invite your students to make two sets of cards that are the same size and color. On the cards of one set, they will write one vocabulary word per card. On the cards of the second set, they will write one vocabulary word definition per card. All cards are mixed together and placed face down on a table. Player #1 then turns over two cards. If the pair matches the word with its definition, the pair of cards belongs to Player #1, and he or she gets another turn. If they don't match, it is another player's turn. Each game player must concentrate in order to remember the locations or revealed words and definitions. The game continues until all matches have been made. The goal of **Vocabulary Concentration** is to match as many words with their definitions as possible. This game works most effectively if it is played in small groups, and is an ideal activity for free exploration time.

❑ Have your students practice their writing skills by creating sentences and paragraphs in which **multiple vocabulary words** are used correctly. Ask them to share their sentences and paragraphs with the class.

❑ Ask your students to create paragraphs which use the vocabulary words to present **History Lessons** that relate to the time period of World War II.

❑ Challenge your students to use a specific vocabulary word from the story at least **10 Times In One Day**. They must keep a record of when, how, and why the word was used!

❑ As a group activity, have students work together to create an **Illustrated Dictionary** of the vocabulary words.

❑ Play **20 Questions** with the entire class. In this game, one student selects a vocabulary word and gives clues about this word, one by one, until someone in the class can guess the word.

❑ Play **Vocabulary Charades**. In this game, vocabulary words are acted out!

You probably have many more ideas to add to this list. Try them. See if experiencing vocabulary on a personal level increases your student's vocabulary interest and retention.

Quiz Time!

1. On the back of this paper, write a one paragraph summary of the major events in each chapter of this section. Then complete the rest of this page.

2. What attitudes do the children have toward living in the old country house?

   _____

   _____

3. What do the children do on rainy days?

   _____

   _____

4. How do Lucy and Edmund get into Narnia?

   _____

   _____

5. Who does Lucy meet in Narnia? What is his problem?

   _____

   _____

6. Who does Edmund meet? What does she offer him?

   _____

   _____

   _____

7. Why does Edmund lie about not being in Narnia?

   _____

   _____

8. What is the weather like in Narnia? Why?

   _____

   _____

   _____

9. Have you ever experienced something odd, and when you tried to tell someone else about it, they didn't believe you? Explain on the back.

Rainy Day Word Game

When Peter, Susan, Edmund and Lucy arrive at the old mansion, they are eager to explore the countryside around it, but unfortunately, it rains. They then decide to explore the old house itself and play hide-and-go-seek. Have you ever been stuck inside on a rainy day? Here is a game you can play in the rain or any kind of weather.

The game requires at least two players. The first player thinks up two rhyming words like "Lincoln, blinken." He announces that he has a "hinky-pinky" (two two-syllable rhyming words.) He then gives a clue like "former president's eyelid movement." The second player then tries to guess the hinky pinky or asks yes or no questions until he can guess it. Once the second player guesses the hinky-pinky, he/she thinks up one for the first player to guess.

Players may also use "hink-pink" (two one-syllable rhyming words) or "hinkety-pinkety (two three syllable rhyming words) riddles. Here are some riddles to help you get started.

1. Bunny's routines are _____
   (hinky-pinky)

2. A truck carrying aluminum containers is a _____
   (hink-pink)

3. An evening illuminator is a _____
   (hink-pink)

4. A humorous rabbit is a _____
   (hinky-pinky)

5. A home-based rodent is a _____
   (hink-pink)

6. A dam-buiding animal's fetcher is a _____
   (hinky-pinkety)

7. Narnia's "queen's" knitting is _____
   (hinky-pinky)

8. A dog's foolishness is a _____
   (hinky-pinky)

The game can be played with the riddles and clues prepared on flashcards to help students get started. Any group of two or more can play. Rhymes can relate directly to the novel or to general knowledge. Try out your own home-made hinky-pinky on your next rainy day!

Trip to Narnia

When Lucy came to Narnia for the first time she met a faun by the name of Mr. Tumnus. This half-man, half-goat carried an umbrella in one hand and several brown packages in the other. He drops his packages when he sees Lucy and then begins to converse with her. They talk and Mr. Tumous invites Lucy to his cave for tea. There, he lulls her to sleep, but then admits he is working for the White Witch and must bring in any humans he finds. He shows her the way back to the wardrobe and they part as friends.

Edmund has a quite different meeting, with the White Witch herself! She meets him as she rides in her sledge, driven by a fat, three-foot dwarf. When the Witch finds out Edmund is human, she is about to turn him to stone with her wand. Then she tries a friendly approach, offering him a hot drink and enchanted Turkish Delight candy. She finds out about the other humans (his brother and sisters) and offers to feed Edmund more Turkish Delight, even make him King of Narnia, if he will just bring them to her castle. Edmund likes the idea, and can't wait to get more candy and lord it over the other kids.

Working in size-appropriate groups, recreate one of these meetings in Narnia. It is up to each group to decide how many players will be needed to present the scene to the class. In the scene you and your group choose to perform, you may change the outcome of the confrontation in any way you wish.

Possibilities include:

- Mr. Tumnus turns Lucy in to the Witch.

- The Witch turns Edmund to stone.

- Edmund and Lucy meet and argue about whether the witch is really Queen of Narnia.

- The Witch shows up while Tumnus and Lucy are talking. They both run away.

A number of scenarios are possible. It is up to you and your group members to decide what type of scene to perform. Remember, no one is to get hurt in any way as you enact your "drama in Narnia."

Villains In Literature

The White Witch is the main villain in *The Lion, the Witch and the Wardrobe*. She rules Narnia in a cold, cruel way by turning her enemies to stone and keeping it winter all the time. If Aslan is the hero, the White Witch is surely the villain.

You may have read or seen a story with a villain. Every superhero has villains to fight against. Batman has the Joker. Superman has Lex Luther. Comic books and cartoons are filled with heroes and villains.

On the chart below, make a list of villains. Beside them, describe what makes them so bad (not just that they fought against the hero). What do they look like? What evil schemes do they carry out or try to carry out?

Villain	Appearance	Evil Scheme

Reading Response Journals

One great way to insure that the reading of *The Lion, the Witch and the Wardrobe* touches each student in a personal way is to include the use of Reading Response Journals in your plans. In these journals, students can be encouraged to respond to the story in a number of different ways. Here are a few ideas.

- Ask students to create a journal for *The Lion, the Witch and the Wardrobe*. Initially, have them assemble lined and unlined three-holed paper in a yarn or brad-fastened "book" with a blank page for the journal's cover. As they read the story, they may draw a design on the cover that helps tell the story for them.

- Tell them that the purpose of the journal is to record their thoughts, ideas, observations, and questions as they read *The Lion, the Witch and the Wardrobe*.

- Provide students with, or ask them to suggest, topics from the story that would stimulate writing. Here are a few examples from the chapters in SECTION 1.

    — Edmund would do anything to get more of his favorite candy, Turkish Delight. Describe your favorite treat.

    — The children in the novel are sent away to live in an old mansion in the country. Have you ever gone away to live in a strange, new place? What was it like?

- After reading each chapter, students can write one or more new things they learned from the chapter. Ask students to draw their responses to certain events or characters in the story, using the blank pages in their journals.

- Tell students that they may use their journals to record "diary-type" responses that they may want to enter. Encourage students to bring their journal ideas to life! Ideas generated from journal writing can be used to create plays, debates, stories, songs, and art displays.

- Allow students time to write in their journals daily.

- Explain to the students that their Reading Response Journals can be evaluated in a number of ways. Here are a few ideas.

    — Personal reflections will be read by the teacher, but no corrections or letter grades will be assigned. Credit is given for effort, and all students who sincerely try will be awarded credit. If a "grade" is desired for this type of entry, you could grade according to the number of journal entries completed for the number of assignments.

    — Nonjudgmental teacher responses should be made as you read the journals to let the students know that you are reading and enjoying their journals.

    — If you would like to grade something for form and content, ask the students to select one of their entries and "polish" it according to the writing process.

Quiz Time!

1. On the back of this paper, write a one paragraph summary of the major events that happen in each of the chapters in this section. Then complete the rest of the questions on this page.

2. Why does the professor say that "we must assume" that Lucy is telling the truth about Narnia?

   _____

   _____

3. How do Peter, Susan, Edmund, and Lucy all wind up in Narnia at the same time?

   _____

   _____

4. Why does Peter call Edmund a "poisonous little beast" when they get to Narnia?

   _____

   _____

5. What has happened to Mr. Tumnus?

   _____

   _____

6. Who is Maugrin?

   _____

   _____

7. What do the children decide to do after leaving Tumnus' cave?

   _____

   _____

8. In a well-written sentence, describe the Beavers.

   _____

   _____

9. Who is Aslan? How do the children react to the mention of his name?

   _____

   _____

10. On the back of this page, predict what will happen to Edmund. Support your ideas.

Who Do You Believe?

None of the children believed Lucy's story when she first got back from Narnia. It was simply too strange to think that another world existed in the back of an old wardrobe! Edmund went there and still tried to pretend it didn't exist.

Have you ever tried to figure out who was telling the truth when two people told you different things? What was the situation?

_____

_____

_____

Did you finally figure out which one was telling the truth? How?

_____

_____

Here is a true/false game to play with your classmates. On a piece of paper, write down two things that never really happened to you and one thing that did happen. Individually, show your list to the teacher with the true event underlined and read them aloud to the class. How many students are able to guess which event really happened?

Students score points by the number of true events that they guess. Let the high scorer explain some logical ways to tell truth from falsehood.

16

Are Beavers Like Humans?

Peter, Susan, Edmund, and Lucy spend a day with Mr. and Mrs. Beaver. They follow Mr. Beaver to his home, eat with him there, and discuss how to help Mr. Tumnus. The Beavers and three of the children then flee for their lives when they notice that Edmund has run away.

Some of the things the Beavers do in *The Lion, the Witch and the Wardrobe* are based on facts about what real beavers do. Other things are pure fantasy. Looking at chapters 7 and 8, as well as a reference book on beavers, list those parts of the story which were based on fact and those that are fantasy.

Fact	Fantasy

Logical Syllogisms

The Professor uses logic to conclude that Lucy actually was telling the truth about Narnia. He explains to Peter, Susan, and Edmund: "There are only three possibilities. Either your sister is telling lies, or she is mad, or she is telling the truth. You know she doesn't tell lies and it is obvious that she is not mad. For the moment, then and unless any further evidence turns up, we must assume she is telling the truth."

Logic is a good way to think in order to come to a conclusion or solve a problem. If you can make two true statements about something, you may be able, logically, to make a third statement, or conclusion. For example, if it is true that "Roses are red," and it is also true that "The flower in Lucy's hand is a rose," then it is also true that "The flower in Lucy's hand is red." Now if the professor's statement, "Lucy is lying, mad, or telling the truth," is a true statement and his second statement, "She doesn't lie and she isn't mad" is true, then his conclusion is also true. Lucy is telling the truth.

Sometimes people draw false conclusions from two statements because the third statement is not connected with the first two in a logical way. Look at these three statements:

All lions roar.
Aslan is a lion.
Aslan is a king.

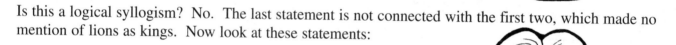

Is this a logical syllogism? No. The last statement is not connected with the first two, which made no mention of lions as kings. Now look at these statements:

All lions roar.
Aslan is a lion.
Aslan roars.

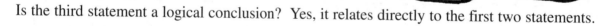

Is the third statement a logical conclusion? Yes, it relates directly to the first two statements.

Which of the following are logical syllogisms and which are not?

1. Peter loves adventures.
   Fighting the Witch is an adventure.
   Peter loves fighting the Witch.

2. Lucy always tells the truth.
   Lucy says she's been to Narnia.
   Lucy is crazy.

3. Church bells ring on Sunday.
   St. Peter's church has bells.
   St. Peter's bells ring Monday.

4. Beavers eat fish.
   Big Tooth is a beaver.
   Big Tooth eats fish.

5. All dogs bark.
   Fido is a dog.
   Fido barks.

6. All cats meow.
   Fluffy is a cat.
   Fluffy purrs.

7. All horses trot.
   Black is a horse.
   Black gallops.

Challenge: For those exercises you thought were not logical, write a conclusion that is logical. Then write a logical syllogism of your own on the back of this paper.

Your Reputation

Lucy had a reputation for telling the truth. Edmund, on the other hand, had a reputation for picking on his younger sister, Lucy, and anyone smaller than himself. Some people have a reputation for being friendly and kind. Others are known to be unfriendly and cruel.

What do you think your reputation is?

_____

_____

_____

Are you more like Lucy or more like Edmund?

_____

_____

Would you like to change your reputation? If so, how?

_____

_____

_____

Do you have a reputation as a good student? Good athlete? If you asked your friends, what would they say you are good at?

_____

_____

What would you like to become good at? How will you achieve your goal?

_____

_____

Quiz Time!

1. On the back of this paper, write a one paragraph summary of the major events that happen in each of the chapters of this section. Then complete the rest of the questions on this page.

2. Does Edmund get to eat more Turkish Delight when he gets to the Witch's house? Why or why not?

   _____

   _____

3. Why do the Beavers and the other three children run away when they discover that Edmund is missing?

   _____

   _____

4. Describe Father Christmas. Why is his appearance a sign that the Witch's spell is breaking?

   _____

   _____

5. What gifts does Father Christmas give? To whom?

   _____

   _____

6. Where is the Witch taking Edmund? Why?

   _____

   _____

7. What does the Witch do when she meets a party of squirrels, satyrs, a dwarf, and a dog-fox?

   _____

   _____

8. What changes are happening in the weather? Why?

   _____

   _____

9. Is Edmund ever going to be King of Narnia? Why?

   _____

   _____

10. On the back of the paper, describe what you see and hear in the springtime where you live. How do you feel when spring comes?

Turkish Delight

Have you ever eaten anything that was so good that you were willing to betray your brothers and sisters to get more? The White Witch found a way to lure Edmund back to her and get him to do what she wanted simply by promising more Turkish Delight, a sugary fruit candy. To make a pan of mouthwatering Turkish Delight you will need the following:

Equipment

- measuring cup
- large heavy saucepan with a cover
- candy thermometer
- large mixing spoon
- 8" (20 cm) square pan
- serving plate
- knife
- stove or hot plate

Ingredients

- $^1/_3$ cup (75 mL) lemon juice
- 3 tablespoons (45 mL) cold water
- rind of one lemon, grated
- 2 tablespoons (30 mL) gelatin powder
- 1 cup (240 mL) of chopped nuts
- $^2/_3$ cup (150 mL) water
- 2 cups (480 mL) sugar
- confectioner's sugar
- butter
- oil

Step 1:

In a measuring cup combine the following ingredients:

- $^1/_3$ cup (75 mL) lemon juice
- 3 tablespoons (45 mL) cold water
- rind of one lemon, grated
- 2 tablespoons (30 mL) gelatin powder

Let stand for at least 5 minutes.

Step 2:

Lightly oil the square pan and sprinkle one cup of chopped nuts into it. Put aside.

Step 3:

Put the saucepan on the stove over moderate heat.

Add:

- $^2/_3$ cup (150 mL) water
- 2 cups (480 mL) sugar

Stir the mixture until the sugar dissolves. Continue heating until boiling starts, then cover and boil 2-3 minutes. Uncover and cook without stirring to 234° F/112° C on the candy thermometer. (This is the soft-ball stage.) Take the pan off the heat and add the gelatin mixture. Place back on the heat and stir until the thermometer reaches 224° F/106° C. Pour the mixture into the square pan. Let it stand for 12 hours.

Step 4:

Butter a knife. Cut into squares. Place candy onto a dish that has been dusted with confectioner's sugar. Dust top with confectioner's sugar.

Scared of Witches?

The White Witch claimed to be the Queen of Narnia. She put a spell on the weather, and turned her enemies to stone with the wave of her wand. Classic children's stories like *The Wizard of Oz, Sleeping Beauty,* and *Snow White* all have witches. In the Middle Ages, many people believed in witches. In the American colonies about 300 years ago, people were burned for practicing witchcraft.

Using an encyclopedia and other books, describe what a witch might look like. Also, find out what witches do and say and find out whether they are always evil. Prepare a report for your class on what your group found out about witches. You could present your report in a number of ways:

- Make a time line of the history of ideas about witches.

- List the names of witches from literature and the stories they come from.

- Draw pictures of witches on a large poster.

- Have members of your group debate, in front of the class, the topic: "Resolved, witches are not real. They exist only in fairy tales."

- Act out a courtroom scene from the Salem, Massachusetts, witchcraft trials.

How Do These Leaders Measure Up?

In *The Lion, the Witch and the Wardrobe,* the White Witch is the evil ruler. Aslan is the true King of Narnia and a good ruler. In history, just as in fairy tales and fictional stories, good and bad kings are found. Often the good kings, or the "true and rightful rulers," fight against the bad kings, or "usurpers."

Using an encyclopedia and other reference books, describe the following leaders.

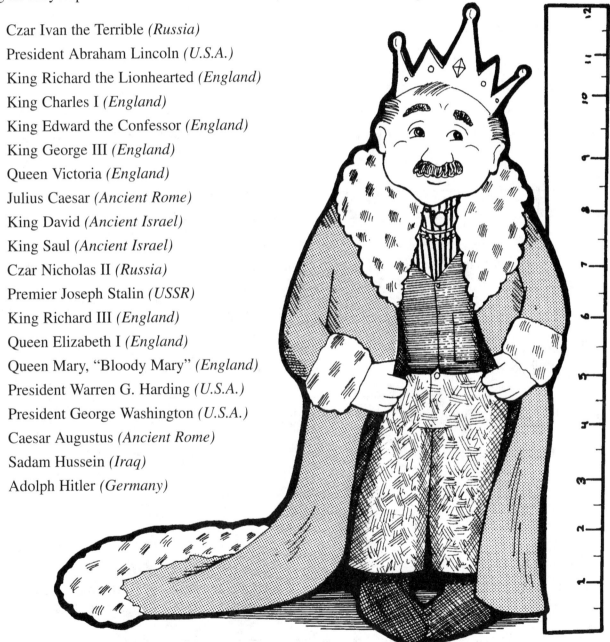

Czar Ivan the Terrible *(Russia)*

President Abraham Lincoln *(U.S.A.)*

King Richard the Lionhearted *(England)*

King Charles I *(England)*

King Edward the Confessor *(England)*

King George III *(England)*

Queen Victoria *(England)*

Julius Caesar *(Ancient Rome)*

King David *(Ancient Israel)*

King Saul *(Ancient Israel)*

Czar Nicholas II *(Russia)*

Premier Joseph Stalin *(USSR)*

King Richard III *(England)*

Queen Elizabeth I *(England)*

Queen Mary, "Bloody Mary" *(England)*

President Warren G. Harding *(U.S.A.)*

President George Washington *(U.S.A.)*

Caesar Augustus *(Ancient Rome)*

Sadam Hussein *(Iraq)*

Adolph Hitler *(Germany)*

Teacher Note: *You may wish to assign an appropriate number of leaders from the list. Also, allow students to find rulers not listed here and classify them as good or bad leaders, so long as they can justify their label with specific facts.*

Temptation

Edmund is the bad boy of the four children. He teases Lucy, lies about having been to Narnia, and tries to betray his brother and sisters to the White Witch in order to get more of his favorite candy and a chance to be King of Narnia.

At some time all of us act like Edmund. We do what we know is wrong. We don't admit it when we know we are wrong because we are too proud. We try to "get back" at our brothers and sisters, make ourselves the leader, or tease someone just because they are younger and we think we can get away with it.

_____

_____

_____

_____

Have you ever done anything to your brothers and sisters that you know was wrong? Why?

_____

_____

_____

_____

Have you ever been tempted to "tell on" or turn in one of the kids you know just to get back at him/her? Describe the situation in 2-3 sentences.

_____

_____

_____

_____

The Witch tempted Edmund with candy and kingship, but gave him neither one. Have you ever been tempted by someone who promised you something? What did they promise? Did they actually give you what they said they would?

_____

_____

_____

If someone were going to tempt you with something, what would it be? A favorite food? Candy? Money? Clothes? Boyfriend or girlfriend? Would you be able to say no to the temptation?

_____

_____

_____

_____

Quiz Time!

1. On the back of this paper, write a one paragraph summary of the major events that happen in each of the chapters in this section. Then complete the rest of the questions on this page.

2. Describe Aslan and the creatures on his side.

   _____

   _____

   _____

3. What does Aslan show Peter? Why?

   _____

   _____

4. How did Peter "win his spurs"?

   _____

   _____

5. List all the creatures siding with the Witch.

   _____

   _____

   _____

6. What does the Witch prepare to do to Edmund?

   _____

   _____

   _____

7. What is the deep magic from the dawn of time?

   _____

   _____

8. What does Aslan do to save Edmund?

   _____

   _____

9. Who are the last two people to see Aslan alive?

   _____

   _____

10. On the back of this paper, tell about someone you know or heard about who sacrificed him/herself to save someone else. (For example: soldiers, crossing guards, police officers, parents, firefighters)

Heroes Today

Peter saved his sister, Susan, from a wolf. Peter "earned his spurs" by heeding the sound of the horn his sister blew and rushing to the scene to slay the attacking wolf. He was a hero. Aslan, already a hero and King in Narnia, makes the ultimate sacrifice to save Edmund, a traitor to his own brother and sisters. Instead of allowing the witch to kill Edmund, Aslan allowed the witch to kill him in Edmund's place.

Begin collecting newspaper articles and magazine articles about heroes today. You may be able to find examples of soldiers, police officers, and firefighters who have rescued someone from a difficult situation. You may even find examples of self-sacrifice in which one person either risks or actually gives up his/her life for another person.

The clippings can be displayed on a bulletin board or in a student-made book entitled "Heroes Today." Students with access to video cameras and VCR machines may want to tape newscasts that show heroic people and then play them for the class.

Some students may prefer to write their own hero stories based on personal experience at home or school. Did one of your parents or friends ever save you from drowning when you waded into water over your head? Have you ever saved your little brother or sister from a bully or a stray dog? Have you ever seen someone save a person in a difficult situation? Write up your hero stories and type them for the classroom or school newspaper.

Narnia Chess

The battle lines in Narnia are being drawn. On the one side are gathered the White Witch, Dwarves, Wolves, Ogres, Cruels, Hags, Incubuses, Wraiths, Horrors, Efreets, Sprites, Orknies, Wooses, and Ettins. On the other we find Aslan, Peter, Susan, Lucy, the Beavers, Tree-Women, Well-Women, centaurs, a unicorn, a bull with the head of a man, a pelican, an eagle, a dog, and two leopards. The great struggle for the Kingdom of Narnia is entering its final act!

The battle for Narnia is not unlike a game of chess (or checkers). Aslan and the Witch can be the opposing King and Queen. Dwarves and Wolves on one side and human children on the other would be the knights and rooks. Fill in the remaining characters as bishops and pawns and you have the ingredients for Narnia chess.

Standard chess pieces with small cardboard nametags taped on for the Narnia characters will help you learn the names of these exotic soldiers. More artistic students may want to create their own chess pieces out of clay or small wood blocks. What does a Cruel look like, anyway? What does Peter look like? Use your imagination to paint or mold your chess pieces to suit your fancy. You may want to use initials instead of full names for your small nametags.

(Teachers may wish to assign one chess piece per student if you are creating original characters. You may wish to have several chessboards, some with original pieces, others merely labeled. Then each small group of students could see a game of chess up close.)

Stone Table Mural

The Stone Table is the gathering spot for all creatures faithful to Aslan. It is also the spot where Aslan allows the Witch and her followers to take his life in exchange for letting Edmund go free. On the Stone Table was an inscription that said every traitor belonged to the Witch as her lawful prey, and that for every treachery she had a right to a kill. Unless she is paid in blood for a treachery, all of Narnia will be overturned and perish in fire and water.

Aslan's pavilion at the Stone Table was also impressive, a large tent that looked like yellow silk with cords or crimson and tent-pegs of ivory: and high above it on a pole a banner, which bore a red rampart lion.

A large wall-sized mural could be drawn and painted to include the entire scene: stone table with inscription, pavilion, and lion banner. Someone may try some fancy calligraphy on the inscription. The tent is simple enough, and the lion banner is a common medieval symbol for royalty and can be traced from an encyclopedia or other reference book. Some of the characters can be added: Aslan, Susan, Lucy, Peter, and Edmund.

Students who have difficulty free-hand drawing characters may photocopy the drawing in the paperback edition of *The Lion, the Witch and the Wardrobe*. Then copy them onto heat-sensitive acetate and project them on to the mural with an overhead projector. There they can be traced, while taking care not to move the projector.

After drawing or tracing the Stone Table battle scene, include the castle Cair Paravel in the distance. Paint the whole mural with bright colors for Aslan's Springtime! Later, when you complete your culminating activities, display some of the "dream house" castles on the edge of your wall or bulletin board.

Every traitor belonged to the Witch as her lawful prey.

Rescue Me!

Peter had the courage to rescue his sister from an attacking wolf by plunging his sword into the wolf and killing it on the spot. Similarly, police officers and soldiers may be called upon to rescue people by using violence against an attacker. We depend on some people, like firefighters, paramedics, and ambulance drivers to save our lives when we are in trouble.

Kids can rescue other people, too. Do you know how? On the left side are situations where people need help. On the right are possible solutions. Place the appropriate letter in the space on the left to match problem and solution. More than one answer may be appropriate.

_____ 1. A friend almost drowns at a pool.

a. Dial 911.

_____ 2. You see a robbery in progress.

b. Help stop, drop, roll them, put blanket on them.

_____ 3. You see someone choke on food.

c. Perform artificial respiration.

_____ 4. A dog attacks your sister.

d. Dial 911, warn residents.

_____ 5. A friend's clothes catch fire.

e. Talk to a counselor.

_____ 6. You know someone who is physically abused at home.

f. Perform Heimlich maneuver.

_____ 7. You see a house on fire.

g. Call child abuse hotline.

_____ 8. A friend is using illegal or harmful drugs.

h. Get person away from the dog.

It is a good idea for students to discuss with their parents and decide what is the best thing to do in difficult situations.

Quiz Time!

1. On the back of this page, write a one paragraph summary of the main events in each of the chapters of this section. Then complete the rest of the questions on this page.

2. What was the deeper magic from before the dawn of time?

   _____

   _____

   _____

3. What do Aslan, Susan, and Lucy do after Aslan revives? Where do they go?

   _____

   _____

   _____

4. Explain what happens at the Witch's house. How is Aslan's power the opposite of the Witch's?

   _____

   _____

   _____

5. Where do Aslan and the "statues" go when they leave the Witch's house? How do they get out?

   _____

   _____

6. What is the decisive moment of the battle?

   _____

   _____

7. How does Edmund prove to be a hero in the battle? Who tells Aslan about this?

   _____

   _____

8. After the battle, what new positions do the children assume?

   _____

   _____

9. How do the children get back to the professor's house in England?

   _____

   _____

10. On the back of this paper, predict what the story would have been like without Aslan. What if Aslan had not come back to life?

Cair Paravel

Peter, Susan, Lucy, and Edmund reigned as kings and queens from the castle Cair Paravel by the sea. You can make your own castle.

Materials: cardboard carton (gift or storage boxes work well); stiff paper or 4 paper towel or toilet paper rolls; tape; crayons or paints; string; scissors; 2 metal nuts

Directions:

- Cut off the top flaps of the box, leaving the bottom and sides in one piece. All around the top of the box cut evenly spaced notches about ¹/₄ of the way down. Push in every other tab (created by the notches).

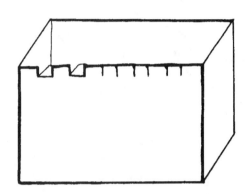

- Make a large door on one side of the carton by cutting an opening to create the door sides and top. Leave the bottom of the door uncut. (The door becomes a drawbridge.) Poke two holes in the wall above the door opening. To reinforce the drawbridge, tape the top and bottom of the fold. Poke a hole in the top corners of the drawbridge. Measure enough string to reach from the opened drawbridge through the top holes in the wall and back to the drawbridge.

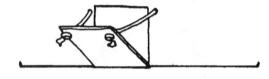

- Next, tie one nut to the end of the string. Push the other end of the string through the bottom of one hole in the drawbridge and then through the hole above the door opening in the cardboard carton on the same side. Push string through the second hole in the carton and then back to the second hole in the drawbridge door. Tie the second nut to the other end of the string.

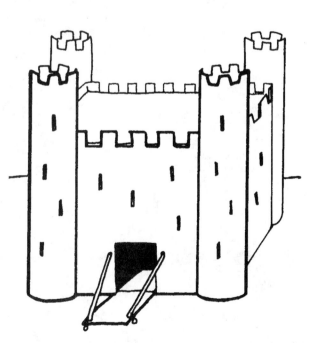

- Use paper towel or toilet paper rolls to create towers. (If carton is very large, roll thin, stiff paper into cylinders.) Cut notches to form a parapet (protecting rampart) in the same way as before. Tape the towers to all four corners of the carton.

- Paint, color, or cover the castle with aluminum foil.

- Color a piece of cardboard or large stiff paper to look like water, and place it under the castle.

- Larger, more complicated castles may be constructed using multiple boxes.

If I Were King or Queen...

The four children, after their victory over the White Witch, reigned as kings and queens of Narnia on the four thrones in Cair Paravel. They managed quite well:

> *"And they made good laws and kept the peace and saved the good trees from being unnecessarily cut down, and liberated young dwarves and young satyrs from being sent to school, and generally stopped busybodies and interferers and encouraged ordinary people who wanted to live and let live. "*

The children all had good reputations as leaders. Peter, a great warrior, was called Peter the Magnificent; Susan was known as Queen Susan the Gentle; Edmund became a great counselor, Edmund the Just. And Lucy became known as Queen Lucy the Valiant.

If you were a king or queen, how would you run things? What kinds of laws would you make? How would you enforce them? How, if there were four of you running the same kingdom, would you get along with the other three?

Work in groups of four students to decide how you would run your kingdom. Decide on the name of your kingdom, what laws you would put into effect, and how you would divide responsibilities among you. What would you like to be called: just, gentle, valiant, or magnificent? Be ready to share your plan with the class.

The King of Beasts

Aslan, the Lion King, is a hero for Narnia. He rallies the forces of good against the evil White Witch. He personally kills the Witch in battle. He breathes life into those creatures which had been turned to stone by the Witch and even offers his own life to save Edmund from death at the hands of the Witch.

Can a lion really be called "king of beasts"? Use encyclopedias and other reference books to find out about real lions.

1. Where do lions (outside of zoos) usually live?

2. How big and how heavy do lions get to be?

3. What is a group of lions called?

4. How many lions generally live together?

5. What do lions eat? How do they get their food?

6. Under what circumstances can lions be dangerous to human beings?

7. What efforts are made to preserve the lion population?

On the reverse side of this page, trace or draw a picture of a male lion.

A Breath of Life

Aslan, the lion, reversed the White Witch's magic by breathing on the creatures she had turned to stone. His breath brought the statues in the courtyard of the Witch's castle back to life. The creatures he revived went on to help him win a glorious victory in the big battle with the witch herself.

How could you help "breathe life" into another person? Here are some suggestions:

- Invite a new student in your class to visit your home, join your club, or play with you.

- Visit an elderly neighbor and take a small gift.

- Make friends with a person who has some disability. Help him/her do his homework or think of another way to get to know that person.

- Do chores for a sick or aging relative: mow the grass, take out the trash, clean up, cook, etc.

- Help out with a local litter clean-up campaign. Recycle aluminum cans and use the money to help a favorite charity.

- Volunteer at a pre-school. You could read to the children or help with projects or snack time.

- Write a letter to someone who is in the service.

Try to think of other ways you could help someone. Do you notice any changes in that person? How does helping others make you feel? Write or tell your class about your experience.

Any Questions?

When you finished reading *The Lion, the Witch and the Wardrobe*, did you have some questions that were left unanswered? Write your questions here.

_____

_____

_____

Work alone or in groups to prepare possible answers for the questions you asked above and those written below. When you finish your predictions, share your ideas with the class.

- Will Aslan ever go back to Narnia again?

- Will the four children ever go back to Narnia again?

- If they do find Narnia again, will it be through the wardrobe?

- Will Edmund be permanently changed into a "good guy"?

- Will the four kids ever convince their parents or anyone else that Narnia is a real place?

- How will their experience in Narnia change the way the kids live in the "real" world?

- What will the attitude of the children be towards animals?

- Will Edmund and Lucy be friends?

- Who will reign in Narnia after the children returned to England?

- Will the children go back to London?

- When will they see the Professor again?

- Is it possible that any of the Narnia creatures will come through the wardrobe and into the Professor's house?

- Is the Witch dead, or only temporarily gone?

- What will happen to the Beavers?

- Will the White Stag ever be caught?

- How is it possible for someone to be good and terrible at the same time?

- Will the children still get a strange feeling when they hear the name Aslan?

- Will any other humans ever get into Narnia?

- Are there any old castles in England or Europe that resemble Cair Paravel?

- Will the children take medieval legends and fairy tales seriously after visiting Narnia?

Book Report Ideas

There are numerous ways to do a book report. After you have finished reading *The Lion, the Witch and the Wardrobe*, choose one method of reporting that interests you. It may be a way that your teacher suggests, an idea of your own, or one of the ways mentioned below.

• See What I Read?
This report is a visual one. A model of a scene from the story can be created, or a likeness of one or more of the characters from the story can be drawn or sculpted.

• Time Capsule
This report provides people living at a "future" time with the reasons *The Lion, the Witch and the Wardrobe* is such an outstanding book, and gives these "future" people reasons why it should be read. Make a time capsule, and neatly print or write your reasons inside the capsule. You may wish to bury your capsule after you have shared it with your classmates. Perhaps one day someone will find it and read *The Lion, the Witch and the Wardrobe* because of what you wrote!

• Come To Life!
This report is one that lends itself to a group project. The group picks out a scene from the story for dramatization, acts it out, and relates the significance of the scene to the entire book. Costumes and props will add to the dramatization!

• Into the Future
This report predicts what might happen if *The Lion, the Witch and the Wardrobe* were to continue. It may take the form of a story in narrative, drama, or visual display.

• Guess Who or What!
This report takes the form of several games of "Twenty Questions." The reporter gives a series of clues, general to specific, about a character from the story, and students guess the identity of the mystery character. After the character has been identified, the same reporter presents another "Twenty Questions" about an event in the story.

• A Character Comes To Life!
Suppose one of the characters in *The Lion, the Witch and the Wardrobe* came to life and walked into your home or classroom. This report describes what this character sees, hears, and feels as he or she experiences the world in which you live.

• Sales Talk
This report serves as an advertisement to "sell" *The Lion, the Witch and the Wardrobe*. You decide which group to target and the sales pitch you will use. Include graphics in your presentation.

• Coming Attraction!
The Lion, the Witch and the Wardrobe is about to be made into a movie and you have been chosen to design the promotional poster. Include the title and author of the book, a listing of the main characters and the contemporary actors who will play them, a drawing of a scene from the book, and a paragraph synopsis of the story.

• Literary Interview
This report is done in pairs. One student pretends to be a character in the story. The other student will play the role of a television or radio interviewer, providing the audience with insights into the character's personality and life. It is the responsibility of the partners to create meaningful questions and appropriate responses.

• The Perfect Gift
For this report, you will be responsible for choosing an appropriate gift for three of the characters from the story. Your gifts must be selected from the items available to you. Describe or draw a picture of each gift, name the person it will be given to, and explain why it is the perfect gift for him or her.

• Standard Form
This report is a standard report in which story elements are defined and supported with examples from the book. Areas to include are plot summary, character analysis, setting description, theme explanation, and a personal evaluation of the story.

Find Out More!

Describe three things you read in *The Lion, the Witch and the Wardrobe* that you want to learn more about.

1. _____

2. _____

3. _____

As you read *The Lion, the Witch and the Wardrobe,* you encountered geographical locations, strange creatures, plants, animals, and medieval ideas. To increase your understanding of the characters and events in the story as well as more fully recognize C.S. Lewis' craft as a writer, research to find out more about these people, places, and things.

Work in groups to research one or more of the areas you named above, or the areas that are mentioned below. Share your findings with the rest of the class in any appropriate form of oral presentation.

- chivalry
- lions
- dwarves
- satyrs
- naiads
- pelicans
- heraldry
- knights
- swords
- witches
- incubuses
- faun
- unicorns
- Middle Ages
- laburnums
- burches
- celandines
- Christianity
- hags

- fairy tales
- kings and queens
- centaurs
- nymphs
- dryads
- eagles
- castles
- fealty
- thrones
- Stonehenge
- stag
- sprites
- Adam & Eve
- primroses
- larches
- crocuses
- snowdrops
- logic

Design Your Own Fantasy Kingdom!

Narnia is a great place to visit. You can go there again when you read the other books in the Chronicles of Narnia series. But why not create your own fantasy kingdom?

- Pick a descriptive name for your kingdom.

- Think of a an interesting way to get from the world that we know to your kingdom.

- What kind of creatures will you find in your new world? Make up some interesting names. Try to draw them.

- Draw a map of your kingdom. Label bodies of water, woods, roads, where your different creatures live, and where your castle is located. (See page 40.)

- Design your own castle. (See page 41.) Check the bibliography for help designing your own medieval dream house!

- Make a list of laws that are important for your kingdom.

- Design a coat of arms to emblazon on your shield, banner, and armor. (See page 39.)

- Think of a title, such as Lucy the Valiant, that would reflect your reputation.

- Describe the major industries and resources in your kingdom. Design the money. Will your picture be on the coins or paper money? What other kingdoms will you trade with?

My Coat of Arms

Inside the banner below, design your own coat of arms. Use a picture that helps identify you and your special kingdom.

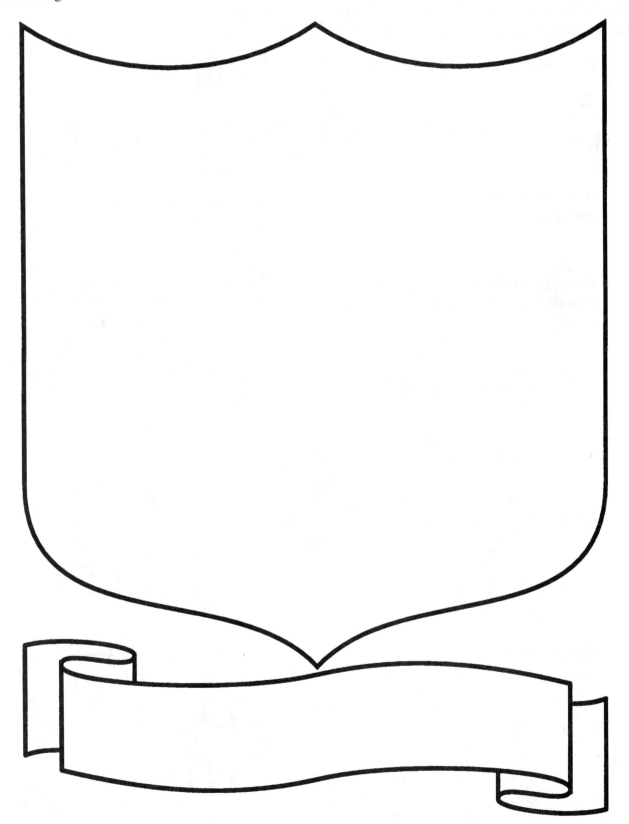

A Map of My Kingdom

On a separate piece of paper, draw a map of your kingdom. You may color code it and include a map key to identify your castle, where your friends live, bodies or water, woods, towns, and roads. Use the symbols below and make up some of your own.

King's Castle

You are a very important person in your kingdom—king or queen. Your house and fortress should be fit for a king. Be your own architect and design the kind of house you have always wanted in the space below.

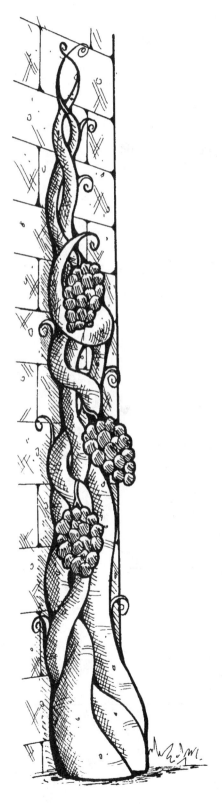
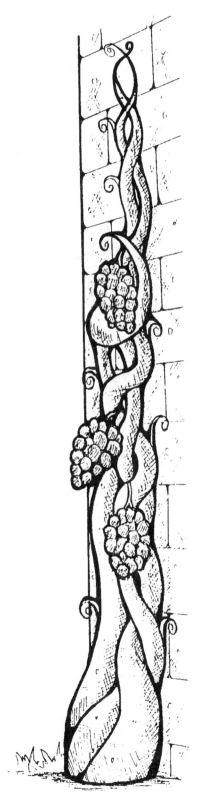

Unit Test

Matching

Match these words with their definitions:

_____ 1. wardrobe

_____ 2. witch

_____ 3. explore

_____ 4. Cair Paravel

_____ 5. lion

a. look around

b. castle

c. Aslan

d. Queen

e. closet

True or False

Write true or false next to each statement below. On the back of this paper, explain why each false answer is false.

1. _____ The White Witch is the true Queen of Narnia.

2. _____ Edmund lies about being in Narnia.

3. _____ Lucy runs from the faun when she sees him.

4. _____ Peter, Susan, and Edmund wonder where Lucy has been for so long.

5. _____ Edmund is tempted by Turkish Delight.

6. _____ Aslan and the Witch fight against the children.

7. _____ The Witch turns creatures to stone.

8. _____ Lucy teases Edmund about Narnia.

9. _____ The four children reign as kings and queens.

10. _____ Peter dies to save Aslan.

Short Answer

Provide a short answer for each of these questions.

1. Who does Edmund meet on his first visit to Narnia?

   _____

2. At first, what is the weather like in Narnia? Why?

   _____

3. What happens to Mr. Tumnus?

   _____

4. List the gifts Father Christmas gives the children.

   _____

5. What is the deep magic from the dawn of time?

   _____

Essay

1. On the back of this paper, explain why Aslan is important to the story.

2. On the back of this paper, describe the changes that take place in Narnia.

Response

Explain the meaning of each of these quotations from *The Lion, the Witch and the Wardrobe.*

Chapter 2: " 'Daughter of Eve from the fair land of Spare Oom where eternal summer reigns around the bright city of War Drobe, how would it be if you came and had tea with me?' "

Chapter 3: "He sneered and jeered at Lucy and kept on asking her if she'd found any other new countries in other cupboards all over the house."

Chapter 4: "The more he ate, the more he wanted to eat."

Chapter 5: " 'Either your sister is telling lies, or she is mad, or she is telling the truth.' "

Chapter 8: " 'He's gone to her, the White Witch. He has betrayed us all.' "

Chapter 10: "It's an old hiding place for beavers in bad times."

Chapter 11: "All the things he had said to make himself believe that she was good and kind and that her side was really the right side sounded to him silly now."

Chapter 12: "People who have not been in Narnia sometimes think that a thing cannot be good and terrible at the same time."

Chapter 15: " 'I feel my strength coming back to me. Oh, children, catch me if you can!' "

Chapter 16: "Then with a roar...the great beast flung himself upon the White Witch."

Chapter 16: " 'It's all right!' shouted Aslan joyously. 'Once the feet are put right all the rest of him will follow.' "

Teacher Note: Choose an appropriate number of quotes for your students.

Conversations

Work in groups to write and perform the conversations that might have occurred in each of the following situations.

- The Witch sees Tumnus escorting Lucy back to the Wardrobe. (3 people)

- Edmund tries to escape from the Witch. (2 people)

- Lucy and Edmund are both caught by the Witch. (3 people)

- Aslan never comes and the children are still trying to rescue Tumnus. (5 people)

- Tumnus and Lucy talk after the battle is over. (2 people)

- Peter and Edmund talk after the battle is over about bravery and apologies. (2 people)

- Mr. Beaver is fighting with the Witch's dwarf and challenging him as they struggle. (2 people)

- Peter and Susan discover a new way to get into Narnia. (2 people)

- Aslan passes out medals for bravery to the children. (5 people)

- Mr. Tumnus goes through the wardrobe into the Professor's house and bumps into Mrs. Macready, the housekeeper. (2 people)

- Superman and Batman join forces with Aslan and plan a strategy against some evil forces. (3 people)

- Peter and Mr. Beaver discuss plans for a new dam that will provide water for a moat around Cair Paravel. (2 people)

- Some dwarves and Orknies that were not totally defeated discuss how to regain control of Narnia. (2 or more people)

- Lucy discusses her upcoming marriage to a neighboring prince. (2 or more)

Bibliography of Related Reading

Gaffron, Norma. *Unicorns.* (Greenhaven, 1989)

Grimm, Brothers. *Sleeping Beauty.* (Harcourt, 1959)

Lang, Andrew. *Blue Fairy Book.* (David McKay, 1948)

Lee, Alan. *Castles.* (McGraw-Hill, 1984)

Lewis, C.S. *The Great Divorce.* (Macmillan, 1946)
    The Horse and His Boy. (Macmillan, 1954)
    The Last Battle. (Macmillan, 1956)
    Letters to Children. (Collins, 1985)
    The Lion, the Witch and the Wardrobe. (Macmillan, 1950)
    The Magician's Nephew. (Macmillan, 1955)
    Mere Christianity. (Macmillan, 1943)
    Miracles. (Macmillan, 1947)
    Perelandra. (Macmillan, 1965)
    The Screwtape Letters. (Macmillan, 1961)
    Surprised by Joy: the Shape of My Early Life. (Harcourt, 1956)

Lurie, Alison. *Fabulous Beasts.* (Farrar Straus Giroux, 1981)

Matthews, John and Bob Stuart. *Warriors of Christendom.* (Firebird, 1988)

Schaller, George and Kay. *Wonders of Lions.* (Dodd, Mead, and Company, 1977)

Starkey, Dinah. *Ghost and Bogles.* (Heinemann, 1985)

Unstead, R.J. *British Castles.* (Thomas Y. Crowell, 1970)
    See Inside a Castle. (Warwick, 1986)

Windrow, Martin. *The Medieval Knight.* (Franklin Watts, 1985)

Answer Key

Page 10

1. Accept appropriate responses.
2. The children are generally positive about the old house, the grounds, and the easy-going old professor.
3. The children explore the house and play hide-and-seek.
4. Lucy and Edmund find Narnia in the back of an old wardrobe.
5. Lucy meets a faun, Mr. Tumnus, who is working for the White Witch looking to capture humans.
6. Edmund meets the White Witch, who claims to be Queen of Narnia, and offers him candy and the chance to be king if he will bring his brother and sisters to her.
7. Edmund did not want to admit Lucy was right about Narnia and he was more than half on the side of the Witch.
8. Narnia always has winter but never Christmas because of the Witch's spell.
9. Accept reasonable responses.

Page 11

1. rabbit's habits
2. can van
3. night light
4. funny bunny
5. house mouse
6. beaver-retriever
7. witch's stitches
8. collie folly

Page 15

1. Accept appropriate responses.
2. Logically, Lucy is either lying, crazy, or telling the truth. She didn't lie, and obviously isn't crazy.
3. Mrs. Macready is leading a tour, and the children, trying to get out of the way, wind up in the wardrobe.

4. Peter realizes Edmund lied about Narnia.
5. Mr. Tumnus is taken captive by the Witch and has his cave ransacked.
6. Fenris Ulf is a wolf and captain of the Witch's secret police.
7. They decide to try and help Tumnus.
8. Accept appropriate responses.
9. Aslan, a lion, is King of the wood and son of the great Emperor-Beyond-the-Sea. The children felt something jump inside when his name is mentioned.
10. Accept reasonable responses.

Page 17

fact: Beavers are small animals that build dams, fish, have paws, fur, etc.

fantasy: Beavers do not talk to humans, use human implements like frying pans, ovens, pipes, etc.

Page 18

Logical syllogisms: 1, 4, 5

Page 20

1. Accept appropriate responses.
2. No. The Witch lied to Edmund, and he didn't deliver his brother and sisters.
3. The Beavers are sure Edmund has gone to the Witch, and they are headed for the Stone Table to join Aslan.
4. Father Christmas is Santa Claus. Since the Witch outlawed and cast a spell against Christmas, his presence is a sign that her power is waning.
5. Peter received a sword and shield; Susan, a bow, arrows, and a horn; Lucy, a healing cordial.
6. She is taking him to the Stone Table to kill him.
7. The Witch turns the whole group to stone.
8. The snow melts, spring arrives.
9. Accept reasonable answers.
10. Accept reasonable responses.

Answer Key *(cont.)*

Page 23

Ivan—bad-cruelty, mass killings

Lincoln—good-emancipation

Richard—good-crusader

Charles—bad—taxation without representation

Edward—good-national defenses, education

George—bad-taxation without representation

Victoria—good-long reign of peace, prosperity

Julius Caesar—mixed-dictator, reformer

David—good-true to God

Saul—bad-disobedient to God

Nicholas—bad-weak leader, indecisive

Stalin—bad-tyrant, killed millions

Richard—bad-took throne by force

Elizabeth I—good-peace, prosperity

Mary—bad-martyred non-Catholics

Harding—bad-Teapot Dome money scandal

Washington—good-war hero, stable

Augustus—good-long reign of peace, prosperity

Hussein—bad-invaded Kuwait

Hitler—bad-killed millions

Page 25

1. Accept appropriate responses.
2. Accept appropriate responses.
3. Aslan shows Peter, from a distance, the castle Cair Paravel because that's where he will reign as king.
4. Peter saves his sister Susan by killing the wolf, Fernus Ulf, who attacks her.
5. Dwarves, Wolves, Ogres, Cruels, Hags, Incubuses, Wraiths, Horrors, Efreets, Sprites, Orknies, Wooses, Ettins
6. The Witch prepares to kill Edmund.
7. For every treachery, the Witch has the right to a kill.
8. Aslan allows the Witch to kill him instead of Edmund.
9. Susan and Lucy are the last two people to see Aslan alive.
10. Accept appropriate responses.

Page 29

1. c, a	2. a	3. f, a	4. h
5. b	6. e, g	7. d	8. e

Page 30

1. Accept appropriate responses.
2. When a willing victim was killed in traitor's stead, the Table would crack and Death itself would start working backwards.
3. They romp and play. The girls ride Aslan to the Witch's house.
4. Aslan breathes on the statues that the Witch turned to stone. They come back to life.
5. The revived creatures go back to the battle with the Witch. A giant breaks down the gate.
6. Aslan roars and personally attacks the Witch.
7. Edmund broke the Witch's wand that she used to turn creatures to stone and was wounded. Peter told Aslan.
8. The children become kings and queens.
9. They entered a thicket to hunt the White Stag and wound up in the wardrobe.
10. Accept appropriate responses.

Page 33

1. Africa.
2. 500 pounds, 3 feet tall at the shoulders, 10 feet long.
3. a pride.
4. About 6.
5. They stalk and kill other animals, especially zebra. Female lions do most of the hunting.
6. Older lions that can't kill wild game may attack humans. They may attack if intruded on during mating season. Lions have killed more humans in Africa than all other wild game combined.
7. Large game preserves are found in Africa.

Answer Key *(cont.)*

Pages 38–41

Create a bulletin board to display these culminating activities.

Page 42

Matching: 1) e 2) d 3) a 4) b 5) c

True or False

1. False; She only claims to be the Queen.
2. True
3. False; She goes to his cave for tea.
4. False; There is no sense of time lost.
5. True
6. False; Aslan fights against the Witch.
7. True
8. False; Edmund teases Lucy.
9. True
10. False; Aslan dies to save Edmund.

Short Answer

1. The White Witch
2. Always winter but never Christmas because of the Witch's spell.
3. He is captured and turned to stone by the Witch.
4. Peter—sword and shield; Susan—bow and arrows, horn Lucy—healing cordial.
5. All traitors face death at the hand of the Witch.

Essay

1. Accept appropriate responses. Include 3 things Aslan does.
2. Accept appropriate responses. Include the weather, new kings, reviving statues.

Page 43

Accept all well-supported answers.

Page 44

Perform the conversations in class. Ask students to respond to the conversations in several different ways such as, "Are the conversations realistic?" or, "Are the words the characters say in keeping with their personalities?"